Images of the Wild

Photography and Stories by
Carl R. Sams II & Jean Stoick

Illustrations by

Michael Glenn Monroe

Edited by

Colleen Monroe

Sleeping Bear Press

Acknowledgments

We would like to thank:

Michael Glen Monroe and his wife Colleen for their special touches. Michael, 1997 Michigan duck stamp winner and featured artist at two of the country's finest wildlife art festivals, contributed the sketches for the book. A free lance writer, Colleen assisted with the editing of our stories.

Bruce Montagne, our art director, for tracking down and organizing our original slides as well as providing suggestions on layout and design.

Cari Cabot, our office manager, for holding things together while we worked on this project.

Sleeping Bear Press
121 South Main
P.O. Box 20
Chelsea, MI 48118

Sleeping Bear Ltd.
7 Medallion Place
Maidenhead, Berkshire
England

Printed and bound in Canada by Friesen's, Altona, Manitoba.

10 9 8 7 6 5 4 3 2 1

Cataloging-in-Publication Data on file
ISBN 1-886947-18-X

Dedication

We dedicate this book to my mother, Elizabeth Margaret Sams, who fed and watched the birds each day from her kitchen window. While still new to Northern Michigan, I remember looking excitedly through a bird guide with my mom, trying to identify the strange, prehistoric-looking bird that we later labeled a great blue heron. She gave me the opportunity to grow up in the North Country, where I explored the woods and waterways, and developed my love for the outdoors.

The memory of her gentle soul and her love for all creatures will be in our hearts forever.

Foreword

My husband, Roger Tory Peterson, and I first met Carl Sams and Jean Stoick in 1993. We had admired their work for years. Roger, a passionate photographer, felt strongly that great photography should be accepted as art.

When Roger wrote the foreword to the book, *Nature Photography: A Current Perspective,* he stated, "Many magazine articles may not be read, but the photographs that accompany them cannot be ignored. Whether they have impact — whether they are 'worth a thousand words' — depends on the skill of the photographer. They range from badly-taken 'point and shoot' pictures, to purely documentary photos, to those of artistic merit imbued with some understanding of composition and the quality of light. At the top of this craft is a photographer like Carl Sams, who gains the added dimension of feeling by spending day after day with the same family of deer or nesting loons."

Images of the Wild is a book Roger would have enjoyed immensely. He knew the many years of commitment that Carl and Jean gave to their subjects. He appreciated the difficulties in capturing animal behavior under special lighting conditions and composing subjects in the right backgrounds. This book is striking proof the authors have mastered these skills.

Carl's and Jean's artistic talent, knowledge of wildlife, and persistence have elevated their photography to another level. It is truly an art form.

Virginia Marie Peterson

Photographic Beginnings

Before I could afford to purchase the necessary equipment, I used to take imaginary photographs of subjects that caught my attention. My wife, Jeannie, a middle school art teacher, knew my love for nature and urged that investing in a camera would give me an outlet for my creativity. In May of 1982, I sold guns and bows for a down payment toward my first Nikon 35mm and signed up for a workshop instructed by John Shaw and Larry West, two of the country's premier nature photographers. I shared the information John and Larry taught me about cameras and photography with Jeannie. She, in turn, taught me the fine points of composition. We then started getting out often to photograph deer, picking up our slides the next day to review our progress. The following day we would go back and correct our mistakes. This instant feedback method led us to many new ideas about how we could take better pictures.

Over the years, we have found that the best pictures are missed not because you forgot to bring your camera, but because you didn't bother to go out and try at all. At the end of each day that we aren't able to photograph, we wonder what magic moments that day we may have missed.

If your goal is to be the very best photographer, you have to be constantly taking pictures. Getting out into the field, shooting film, and having a firm understanding of your subjects is the only way to provide yourself with the opportunities to truly capture *Images of the Wild.*

Milkweed Buck

On a still, warm afternoon in late October, Jeannie and I picked up our cameras and
headed out in search of wildlife to photograph before the fall colors faded. This little button
buck was one of three fawns born to the white-tail family that we had been photographing
for several years. On this day, as usual, he was the first to notice and investigate our arrival.
When he began to approach us, I tried to reposition myself to line him up with the rust color
of the oak leaves behind him. Just as I was making my move, he walked into a dried
milkweed plant, which exploded, sending fluffy seeds drifting through the air about his head.

We began to click off film, excited about the image. I could hear Jeannie working from
another angle, counting out her shots slowly, "...thirty-six...thirty-seven...thirty-eight..." She
stopped. Her roll of film should have been finished by then. She popped open her camera
back to discover that there was no film inside! I swallowed hard realizing that I had used
that camera the day before and had forgotten to reload it.

That afternoon, I often tell people, was one of my most dangerous times in the field.

This photo became our trademark, which opened the doors for us to dive into the art and
nature world market. The "Milkweed Buck" was the cover for *Terre Sauvage* magazine in
France and the cover of *Airone* in Italy.

The Bison

Bison are mistakenly thought to be very docile animals, grazing and meandering slowly across the grasslands. However, weighing well over 2,000 pounds, they account for many serious injuries in the National Parks. The beauty of the giant bison should be viewed from afar.

Elk and Evergreen

In Yellowstone National Park, under the cover of an early morning fog, I waded through the icy waters of the Gibbon River, following the shrill bugle of a bull elk. Suddenly, I turned to witness the massive bull ferociously tearing up a patch of evergreens with his antlers. With no tree near enough to hide behind, I dropped to the ground and began to photograph. Looking around I realized that there were two herds uncomfortably close together. A cow elk bolted from one harem to another before her bull was able to turn her back. Thus, the two large bulls squared off and I moved even closer to get myself into position to shoot the fight that might ensue. They turned, charged, and hit with such a tremendous impact that it forced their legs out from under them. Mud and dirt were flying as they lost their balance and catapulted toward me, completely out of control. Finding myself entirely too close for comfort, I ran backward to escape, clutching camera and tripod, still taking pictures.

Coyote

During early October in Yellowstone National Park, I spotted this young coyote trotting toward me in his new winter coat. My first instinct was to raise my tripod to avoid shooting through the grasses, but I decided against it, not wanting to startle him. Preoccupied with his search for field mice, he came within range, still unaware of my presence. By making a slight noise, I caught his attention and squeezed the shutter.

Artistically, I like this image because of its shallow depth of field and the blend of warm and cool colors.

Sharp-Tailed Grouse

While on assignment for *Audubon* magazine in the Upper Peninsula of Michigan, I came across what appeared to be sharp-tailed grouse feathers and droppings scattered over a large circular area — evidence of a dancing lek. I marked the spot on my map, made a note on my calendar, and went there in late April the following year when the mating ritual takes place. Working from a blind built within a giant stump, I camped out at the site so I could be set up and in place long before the grouse would come in. A heavy frost covered the ground, and as the sun's rays lifted, the males danced and sounded off to draw in the females. They strutted the instinctive mating ritual that inspired many aspects of Native American dances. It was the most memorable mating ritual I have ever witnessed.

Fox Trot

These two little foxes belonged to a family of four kits we photographed in Ontario along Lake Superior's north shore. The two siblings were about the same body weight and frequently came up with new wrestling holds to use on each other. We called this pose the "Fox Trot," not just because it resembled the dance, but also because of how the daisy resembles a boutonniere on the chest of the one partner.

Chipmunks and Acorns

Every photographer has a personal wish list of photographs that he or she would like to take someday. One of mine had always been a chipmunk with bulging cheeks full of acorns. The problem I encountered during the fall was that there were so many acorns, I could never isolate the chipmunk. So, I waited until a time when nuts were less abundant and found this little fellow looking for extras after he had diminished his winter stash. He stuffed an acorn into each cheek and then left frustrated that he couldn't carry off a third!

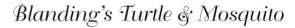

Blanding's Turtle & Mosquito

Early one spring I was working with a herpetologist on an article about snapping turtles. Driving down a two-track trail in Hell, Michigan, we braked for a Blanding's turtle that was crossing in front of our pickup. I got out, crouched down low, and pushed my tripod along as I inched toward the terrified turtle. As I was setting up my shot, a cloud of mosquitoes hovered around my head and one landed on the nose of the turtle and filled up. We both gave our share of blood for that shot.

Showy Lady's Slippers

On June 20th, Jeannie and I drove slowly around back roads in the Pigeon River country of northern Michigan, hoping to find some elk to photograph. Scanning the woods as we drove, Jeannie thought she saw a bit of litter left behind by careless hikers and asked if I would pull over so we could clean it up. We stopped, wandered into the swamp, and stood in amazement as we realized that our "trash" was an entire patch (over an acre) of Showy Lady's Slippers.

Foot Waggle Loon

Loon chicks learn quickly to mimic their parents with their clumsy attempts to dive, their rolling over to preen their bellies, and their awkward wing flaps. The young loon on the opposite page is demonstrating the "foot waggle," a classic behavior in which the loon will stretch out his leg to rotate and shake his foot. Jeannie and I saw this behavior several times during the day, usually after the loons had been well fed and were about to settle down for a nap.

Black Bear and Triplet Cubs

During the last week of April, we received a tip that triplet bear cubs had been spotted in Seney National Wildlife Refuge. Seney, with its 152 square miles, is the biggest refuge east of the Mississippi. We went out searching for most of an entire day but could not locate any action. As our day was coming to a close I did see one adult bear, but no cubs.

The next evening we decided to give it another try. Driving back into the refuge, we were flagged down by some researchers who said they had spotted the triplets climbing up a tree in the same area we had seen the large bear the day before.

Knowing the danger of getting between a sow and her cubs, we decided to try to use the car as a blind. We entered a clearing and saw the large bear bedded next to a tall pine tree in the back of the field. We approached slowly in the vehicle, expecting her to run off, but she held her ground as we came within thirty-five yards — but — still no cubs.

I extended my tripod and leaned out the window of the truck to photograph the mother, thinking to myself that if this massive animal were to charge we would drive off leaving our equipment behind.

While photographing, I saw her glancing upward several times before I realized she was checking on her 3 cubs high up in the towering white pines.

Bobolink on Territory

The bobolink is often identified by his "reverse tuxedo" markings. In an overgrown farm field, this male and several others used to land on the tallest weeds and sing loudly to claim their territory. I snapped this photo in the third week of June while scouring the rough meadows and unplowed fields, looking for birds to photograph.

The bobolink has the second longest migration path of any bird in North America. It has been discovered that this bird has a magnetic compass field in its head and knows the direction of true North.

Fighting Egrets

Great egrets nest in close proximity to one another, but still defend small territories from intruders of the same species. I noticed that when an egret landed too close to another's nest site, aggressive behavior occurred. One would often attack and chase off the intruder.

Due to windy conditions the day this photo was taken, the birds were held up in the air a while longer, giving me time to anticipate and capture the peak of the action.

Skippers on Sweet Pea

The sweet pea grows wild in the ditch banks along the side of many back roads in rural Michigan. Early in the morning, still laden with dew, the skippers sat motionless as their wings slowly dried out. The colors of the dawn were softly muted and the sweet peas had an iridescent glow about them.

Swan Lake

While finishing up our "Loon Magic" book, we returned to visit a pair of common loons that had chosen a floating platform as their nesting site. On this morning, Jeannie and I were unable to locate them because of a heavy mist, so we drifted along in our kayaks with a family of mute swans. The proud male on guard was gliding out in front with his wings lifted.

Later that day, while photographing the loons, our attention was drawn back across the lake to the male swan, who was creating a ruckus because of something beneath the water. The female swan quickly herded her cygnets up onto the nearby loon nesting platform to keep them out of harm's way. We paddled over to find that the male, in order to protect his young family, was striking at two snapping turtles below the surface of the water.

A Day in the Field with Roger Tory Peterson

During a stay in Florida, I was invited to go on a photo shoot with Roger Tory Peterson. While driving to pick him up, I thought of how nice it would be to take a long ride to Arcadia and photograph some very cooperative scrub jays and meadowlarks I had stumbled onto earlier that week. When I picked Roger up, I expressed my concern that the wind was too strong to photograph near the Gulf, and maybe we should head inland instead. He agreed, and so began our adventure. After arriving and scanning the scene for a while, I asked Roger if I could take a picture of him in the field, using his *Eastern Field Guide.* Sure enough, the moment he opened the book for my photo, one confident scrub jay flew in, hoping for a handout, and landed right on his hand! Memories of that day still make me smile.

In Memory of Roger

I first became acquainted with the authoritative work of Roger Tory Peterson in the seventh grade, when I purchased my first bird field guide to identify an indigo bunting. Roger was the inventor of the field guide and the author of 47 different nature editions over the years. At 85, he was a major force in the formation of the North American Nature Photographers Association.

With his passing at 88, the world lost an accomplished artist, an enthusiastic photographer, and most importantly, a tireless teacher. His bird guides provided the inspiration for my, as well as countless others' wildlife education.

I feel proud to name him my first teacher of nature, fortunate to have had the opportunity to share time with him in the field, and privileged to have called him my friend.

forty

Audubon Cover Doe

One July morning, Jeannie and I waited for this doe to move toward the cool, shaded spot where she often bedded down for the day. We focused our cameras on a nearby spider web and hoped that she would pass by close enough to it so that we could get her and the web — in focus — in the same frame. We held our breath as she approached, knowing that if she were to bump any of the wild bergamot flowers supporting the web, the web would break and the entire composition we were hoping for would be lost. She moved by perfectly, without bumping anything, and this image became our first national magazine cover for *Audubon.*

Foxy Lady

This little fox was one of four fox kits we photographed on the north shore of Lake Superior around the end of June. A colorful array of wildflowers was scattered through the meadows and woodlands, providing a perfect background.

"Foxy Lady" was selected as the image for the 1997 poster for the Northern Wildlife Expo held in Lansing, Michigan.

A Secret Spot

My friend Greg Murray, a wildlife artist, took me to one of his secret fishing spots in central Florida. We were in his boat, moving slowly along the shoreline, when we came across this majestic great blue heron in front of Spanish moss. The cypress swamp was one of the most wondrous areas of Florida I had ever seen.

Light as a Feather

On a pond across from a rookery where several birds had nested on a small island, fish were coming to the surface as if there were no oxygen in the water. A mixed group of great blue herons and great egrets were caught up in a feeding frenzy, swooping down over the water. The great blues struggled awkwardly in mid-air as they tried to catch the fish, while the great egrets gracefully snared one fish after another without missing a wing beat.

Dall Sheep Ram

As a wildlife photographer, I don't feel that animals are the most dangerous things you can encounter in the wild. At times, Mother Nature and her elements can be far more life-threatening.

My friend David Merzel and I, with our camera gear strapped to our backs, climbed in search of a small herd of rams which had been hanging out near a natural mineral lick. A light snow that had fallen the night before covered the ground and made our hike a challenge. As we were nearing the top of the ridge, we mistakenly cut across a scree field (an area of loose shale), slipped, fell, and skidded down the side of the mountain for what seemed like an eternity. Finally, I regained control and started back up the incline, thinking all the way that David was still by my side. At the top, a proud ram was resting on a ledge to warm himself in the sunlight. With adrenaline pumping, I started taking pictures, then I turned to give a "thumbs-up" to my friend, but was surprised to see that he wasn't there. Soon after, up climbed David, exhausted, with bleeding hands, grumbling to ask why I hadn't answered his calls for help.

I am sure it was because of the thin mountain air that I had missed his shouts... or possibly I was just too entranced with this stunning scene.

Pheasant On The Fence

I had just finished speaking to a biologist at a research station when he asked if I'd like to take a few photographs of a pheasant. He sent me down a two-track trail that led back to a wooded lot, a clearing, a broken-down fence, and an abandoned old barn. A few seconds after my arrival a pheasant jumped up onto the fence and sat primping. Leaping out of the van, I grabbed my equipment, turned, and nearly tripped over the pheasant, who was now standing right at my feet. I sat on the ground and squeezed off a couple rolls of film but had to call it a day much earlier than usual, due to the lack of light. My feathered friend was so upset to see I was planning to leave, he flew directly at me to prevent me from getting into the vehicle, and then chased me down the trail as I left.

The biologist never told me the whole story behind the overly-friendly ring-necked pheasant, but you might say that this experience was any wildlife photographer's dream.

Cinnamon Phase Black Bear

I took this photo as I watched the cinnamon bear
wander down the Gardner River in Yellowstone National
Park. She was walking rather aimlessly, stripping rose
hips from the shrubs along the banks.

I photographed her for four days as she fed off a mule
deer carcass she had recently pulled from the water.
During that time, she kept close to the remains, covering
it with sticks and leaves whenever she wasn't feeding.
The river served as a barrier, providing me with a
generous comfort zone to take pictures in.

A fly fisherman didn't heed this comfort zone. As he
approached too closely, the bear charged, rousting him up
out of the river.

Mule Deer Buck

Waterton Lakes National Park

Alberta, Canada

Fighting Mule Deer

On Christmas Day in the Canadian Rockies of Alberta, we came upon two mule deer bucks chasing after a doe. We photographed them locking antlers and fighting for several hours. At one point, they wrestled so close that Jeannie had to grab her camera and back away to a safer spot.

Northern Lights & the Big Dipper

We hiked back eight miles in the bitter cold after a day of photographing moose in Denali National Park, Alaska. It was late August, three feet of snow had fallen, and a cold front that had moved through cleared the skies.

At 11:15 p.m. it became dark enough to see the emerging Northern Lights. They began in the north sky and spread all the way down to the south, as far as the eye could see.

The hair on my arms was standing up for more than one reason that night. It was eleven degrees out, we were down near the river where we had previously watched grizzly bears digging for roots, and we were witnessing the most spectacular display of the Aurora Borealis we had ever seen.

Of all our Alaskan photographs, this is the one I like most. My friend Michio Hoshino, who had camped nearby, shared with us his exposure for photographing the Northern Lights. I owe this image to him as he gave me the details for my camera settings.

Jeannie and I would like to dedicate this page in our book to Michio. He was killed in August of 1996 when he was pulled from his tent by a grizzly bear in Russia. In our opinion, he was one of the top five wildlife photographers in the world. He was always out there... and that's what it takes to be the best. As his images live on, he will be an inspiration to us always.

Moose Bedded in Snow

These two pictures were taken just a few moments apart. A large gust of wind picked up and knocked piles of snow off the branches overhead, completely changing the mood of the image.

Fighting Wolves

It was the third week of February, the peak of the breeding season for wolves in the Upper Peninsula of Michigan. Four feet of snow on the ground made snowshoes a requirement. As I waited near a deer carcass, I spotted a black female coming in to feed, with two males chasing after her, both very excited as she was in heat. One male got a bit frisky with her and the Alpha male did not appreciate it. He forced the would-be suitor into submission, but not before the female (hidden between the two males) put her paw in between them to try to protect the one who had shown his affections.

Porcupine "Tina"

The photo of this porcupine was taken after the sun had dropped down below the horizon. As I approached her, I expected she would turn and raise her quills or run and climb the nearest tree to avoid our interaction. Instead, she relaxed and posed there next to the elk antler she had been munching on.

I decided to adjust my exposure for her dark face, not concerned with how bright it would make the snow in the background. Using a shutter speed of 1/8th of a second, I cautiously clicked off a roll of film until it was too dark to keep shooting. Had she moved even slightly, at such a slow shutter speed, the photo would have been blurred.

The image was introduced as a print at the Northern Wildlife Expo in Lansing, Michigan, where one of my customers labeled the porcupine "Tina" for her Tina Turner-like hairdo. It put a smile on each of our faces, and the title has affectionately stuck ever since.

Blue Jay in the Oaks

As a boy I learned to recognize the calls of the noisy blue jay, the tattletale messenger of the forest. With their loud piercing cries, they often gave me away as I entered the woods. As a photographer, I have grown to appreciate these spirited birds that have clued me in to other creatures moving through their territory, giving me the chance to ready my camera. On one morning I followed their calls to a family of white-tails eating acorns beneath the oaks... acorns which the jays claimed as their own.

Snow Angel Deer

One foggy morning in early March, I went out to search for deer to photograph. I struggled with my equipment through the woods and fields, growing frustrated because I couldn't find a single subject to shoot. About ready to give up, I cut back across the frozen lake and turned to see five deer standing on the ice. I maneuvered cautiously to line up my shot and then dropped to my knees with my tripod close to the ice surface and quickly focused my lens. I whistled twice in an attempt to get them all to turn before they broke the line and spread apart. When they didn't respond, in desperation I flipped over onto my back and made "snow angels" on the ice. The sound of my winter coat scrapping against the ice caught their attention and the deer froze in their tracks — convinced that I had lost my mind! Thus came the title "Snow Angel Deer."

If I judged all the pictures I have ever taken, this would take first place as the most difficult. All it would have taken is for one of the deer to have been one foot closer or further away and it would have been out of the plane of focus. The image would have been lost.

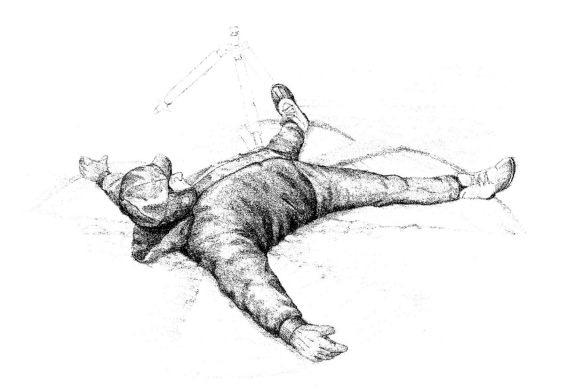

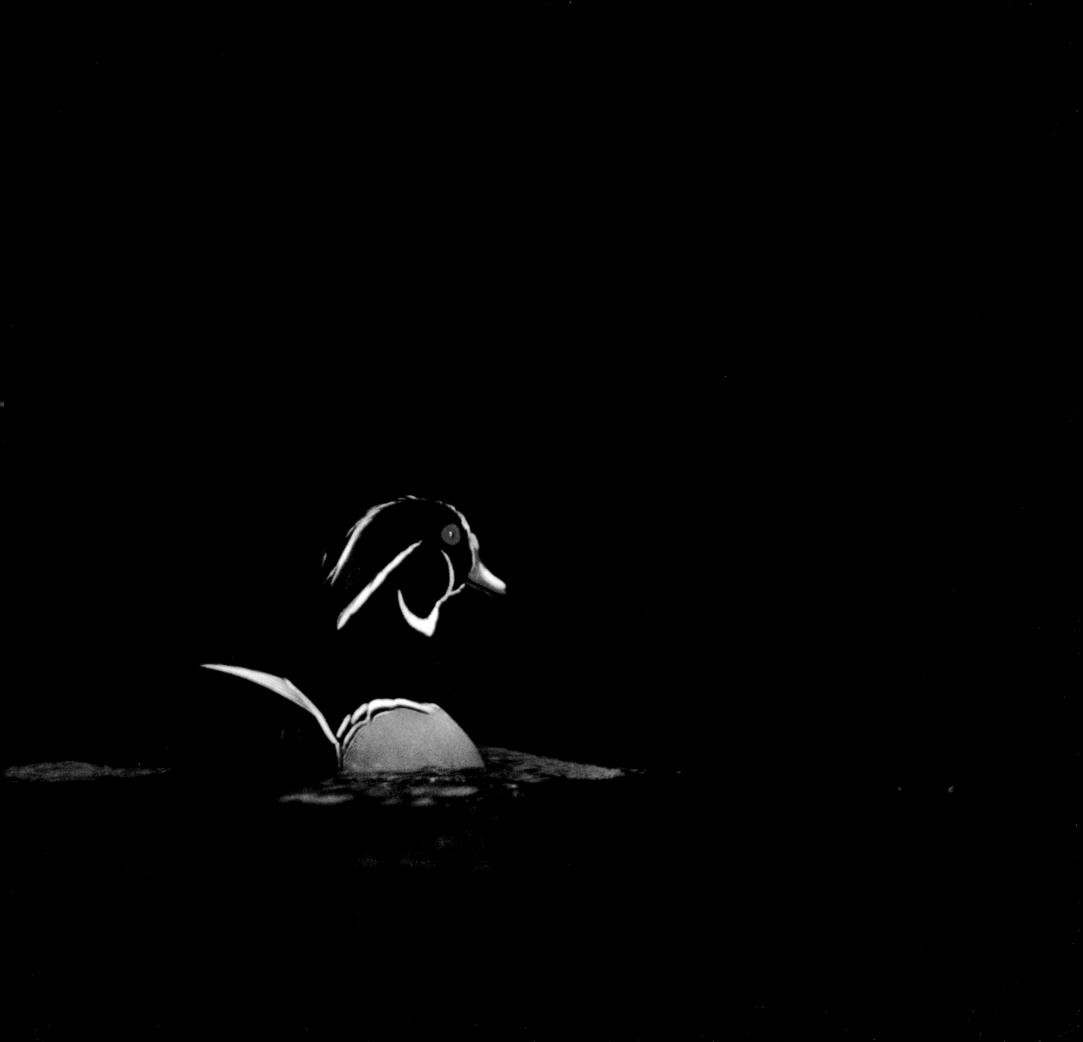

Thirteen-Lined Ground Squirrel

    After spending an entire morning photographing deer, I was heading out of the woods and saw a thirteen-lined ground squirrel munching on dandelion greens. As I approached, he scurried down his hole. I set up my tripod low to the ground so, when he reappeared, I would be at his level. After 20 minutes, he did reappear and started to chew on a dandelion stem, chewing right down to the fluff.

The Pepper Tree

The fast-growing pepper tree has rapidly taken over large areas in numerous parts of the South. Many people feel a serious concern, regardless of the beauty it provides, that it threatens several native plants. The bright red berries are eaten by a wide variety of birds, including the American robin, who cannot digest the seeds, resulting in the rampant spread of the plant.

Out of the Shadows

It was the first week of October in the Upper Peninsula of Michigan when I saw this wolf making his way along the shadowed side of a high ridge. I wondered how I could ever get a shot off with the light levels in the woods as low as they were. As he moved within range, it was looking bleak. My shutter speeds were at about 1 second, much too slow to have any chance of the photo turning out. Just then, as if I were meant to catch this shot, the sun rose high enough to clear the ridge and lit the area the wolf was about to move through. As he walked into the patch of light, I took a spot meter reading on him, focused, and clicked the shutter.

Wings of Freedom

I was doing an art show in Sarasota, Florida when a local fisherman suggested that I might like to try to photograph a bald eagle near Port Charlotte. He told me about a deadwood tree that he had seen one land on several times during the day.

I set up my blind a short distance away from the tree and waited. On the fourth day, as I was taking a meter reading through my lens, she flew in, filling the frame.

This photograph is of a female eagle. Her mate was much smaller than she, as is the case with most raptors.

Prince of the Forest

It was November 6th, the peak of breeding season for white-tailed deer. I went out that particular morning to look for the ten-pointer who had returned as the dominant buck for the second year in a row. Early that morning, I circled through the meadows and wood lots searching for the him, but had no luck. I was about to leave the woods, when a young doe came running towards me. She was so concerned with the buck who was chasing behind her, that she completely ignored me, allowing me to follow them until sunset.

This photo was taken as the last rays of the sun were hitting the tree tops. I positioned myself with the sun at my back and the doe right in front of me. I checked the exposure and held my breath, hoping the buck would follow her and move through the ray of light — and he did just that!

I named this photograph after Bambi's dad, "Prince of the Forest." Its dramatic lighting and the fall colors make this one of my most treasured white-tailed buck photographs.

Carl and the Chickadees

On a perfect October day in 1982, for the first time, a chickadee landed on me. It was startling to have a tiny creature trust me enough to come and claim the sunflower seeds I was holding in my hand. The touch of his tiny feet and weightless body left a lasting impression.

Since then, tufted titmice, downy woodpeckers, and white-breasted nuthatches have all learned to seek me out in the woods to snatch a few of the seeds which I always carry in my vest pocket.

First Snow

One October 19th, the weatherman had predicted a cold front that would move in and bring a snowfall. What he neglected to say was that the storm would start out as rain and sleet, and then change to snow. Thinking that I might be able to photograph deer in the falling snow and fall colors, I made a point to go out into the field even earlier than usual that day. Several hours into my adventure, I was thoroughly soaked, waiting for large flakes to finally begin to fall and whiten the landscape.

This fawn was racing about, electrified with excitement as she approached her yearling mother. I took one picture and immediately realized that the camera had run out of film. I headed for the car, nearing hypothermia, not knowing if the image would turn out. That last shot could have easily been only a half of a frame. Just one snowflake could have blurred the deer's eye. The view finder was so wet and fogged that I wasn't sure if I had hit the focus. But, when the slide came back I could see that the shot was so crisp, even the chin whiskers were sharp!

This picture took First in the World in the Wildlife Behavior category of the British Broadcasting Company's Wildlife Photographer of the Year competition in 1994.

Loons in the Mist

While photographing in Northern Michigan, Jeannie set me up in a floating blind and began to paddle away, just as this pair of loons came out of the mist and swam in between us. She stopped her paddle in mid-air and let them choose their path. As this was our second year with them, the loons felt very comfortable with us. However, the acceptance level of loons varies considerably, and boaters should not approach them, for most will become very upset. This stress is demonstrated when they tremolo and (if they are extremely disturbed) when they splash wildly doing what is called "The Penguin Dance." Unfortunately, many people have mistaken this for what they believe to be a mating dance. Loons do not have a mating dance. This behavior occurs when they are approached too closely.

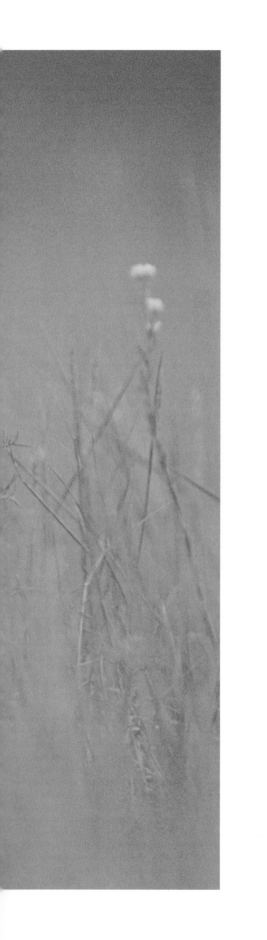

Mule Deer Bucks and Magpie

Jeannie and I spent eight days following three mule deer bucks in the Canadian Rockies. On the morning we took this shot, we couldn't find them anywhere and were about to give up completely when Jeannie spotted the bucks bedded down in tall grass on a hillside more than two miles away. They were so far off that I had to ask her to point out which hill she spotted them on.

We had just gotten over to where they were, when a magpie landed on one of the larger bucks to glean off insects. When it had finished, the magpie went straight for the little spike who was traveling with them. Unnerved by the bird's choice of landing spot, the little one went into a panicked bucking frenzy.

Investing large amounts of time with the same individuals in order to learn about their behavior is essential to create the opportunities to witness and capture these unique events.

Evening Lace

In the 1920s, egrets' tail feathers were used to adorn women's hats, a fad which nearly forced the birds into extinction. As a response, the Audubon Society was formed as an organization which funds protection programs for egrets, and many other species, before they are gone forever.

I spent six springs in Florida before I was finally able to capture this great egret, "Evening Lace," in its full splendor, backlit by the sun. I waited until evening, when the sun was setting and the egret had perched at the top of its rookery. As he dipped down, I snapped the shot, just a split-second before he moved back upward with his head.

Morning Jewel

This image was taken at the same island rookery as the great egret shown on the opposite page. I photographed the great blue heron on a February morning as he stepped out to catch the first warming rays of the sun.

M. MONROE

are places where one can witness herds of bison thundering across the plains, sparring mule deer bucks in a rut, great bears foraging for berries, and bighorn sheep lambs with wobbly legs following their mothers.

One cannot help but realize just how invaluable these spaces are while scanning the horizon, looking out over the expansive forests and mountain ranges dotted with deep blue glacier lakes. Experiencing even a fraction of the beauty held here forces one to understand how important it is to protect these natural areas.

Throughout history, nature photography has played a key role in influencing the public and our politicians to secure and protect our National Parks. We feel, as professional wildlife photographers, that it is not only important, but our responsibility to carry on this tradition.

Photograph Index

69	Moose in Snow Storm Bedded	Denali NP Alaska	300mm	1/125	f 4.5	K64
70	Black Wolf in Birch	Upper Peninsula Michigan	300mm w/1.4x	1/60	f 4	Fuji 100
71	Fighting Wolves	Upper Peninsula Michigan	300mm w/1.4x	1/250	f 4	Fuji 100 Pushed to 200
72	Elk in Frost	Yellowstone NP Wyoming	300mm	1/125	f 4	Fuji 100 Pushed to 200
72-73	Snow Covered Trees Background	Yellowstone NP Wyoming	80-200mm	1/15	f 8	Fuji 100 Pushed to 200
73	Mountain Lion Cub	Montana	500mm	1/8	f 4	Fuji 100 Pushed to 200
73	Blue Eyes	Montana	300mm	1/8	f 2.8	Fuji 100 Pushed to 200
74	Porcupine Tracks	by Michael Monroe	Pencil Sketch			
75	Porcupine	Montana	80-200mm	1/8	f 5.6	Fuji 100
76	Blue Jay in the Oaks	Michigan	300mm w/1.4x	1/60	f 5.6	K64
76	Oak Leaf with Frost	Michigan	200micro	1/60	f 5.6	K64
77	Icy Oak Tree	Michigan	80-200mm	1/30	f 8	K64
78-79	Morning Doves on Snowy Branch	Michigan	500mm	1/125	f 4	Fuji 100 Pushed to 200
80	Carl in Snow Angel Form	by Michael Monroe	Pencil Sketch			
80-81	Snow Angel Deer	Michigan	80-200mm	1/125	f 2.8	K64
82-83	Wood Duck Drake	California	300mm w/1.4x	1/125	f 4	Fuji 100 Pushed to 200
84-85	Buck in Velvet Backlit	Michigan	300mm	1/250	f 2.8	Fuji 100
85	Single Showy Lady Slippers	Michigan	200micro	1/60	f 5.6	K64
86	Tree Frog in Grass	Michigan	200micro	1/30	f 4	Fuji 100
86	13-lined Ground Squirrel	Michigan	80-200mm w/2x	1/125	f.6	K64
87	Mother Goose	Michigan	200micro	1/30	f 5.6	Fuji 100
88	Indigo Bunting on Thistle Inset	Michigan	500mm	1/125	f 4	Fuji 100
88	American Goldfinch in Thistle	Michigan	500mm	1/500	f 4	Fuji 100
88-89	Thistle Back	Michigan	500mm	1/500	f 4	Fuji 100
89	Jeannie in Thistle	Michigan	500mm	1/125	f 4	Fuji 100
90	Swans Taking Off	Michigan	300mm	1/1000	f 2.8	Fuji 100 Pushed to 200
91	Swan Drinking at Sunset	Michigan	300mm	1/1000	f 2.8	Fuji 100 Pushed to 200
92	Fox Pups Hugging	Michigan	500mm w/2x	1/250	f 8	Fuji 100 Pushed to 200
92-93	Abandoned Farm House	N Manitou Island Michigan	80-200mm	1/60	f 5.6	Fuji 100
94-95	Barn Silhouette at Sunrise	Michigan	80-200mm	1/125	f 8	K64
95	Deer Mouse Silhouette	Michigan	200micro	1/125	f 4	K64
96	Robin and the Pepper Tree	Florida	500mm	1/60	f 4	Fuji 100
97	Great Egret Silhouette	Florida	500mm w/2x	1/500	f 8	Fuji 100 Pushed to 200
98-99	Out of the Shadows	Upper Peninsula Michigan	500mm	1/125	f 4	Fuji 100 Pushed to 200
100-101	Wings of Freedom	Florida	500mm	1/1000	f 5.6	Fuji 100 Pushed to 200
102	Prince of the Forest	Michigan	300mm	1/125	f 2.8	Fuji 100 Pushed to 200
103	Red Squirrel on Antler	Michigan	300mm	1/125	f 4.5	K64
104-105	Carl and the Chickadees	Michigan	80-200mm	1/125	f 2.8	Fuji 100
105	Tufted Titmouse	Michigan	300mm	1/125	f 2.8	Fuji 100 Pushed to 200
105	Black Capped Chickadee	Michigan	300mm	1/125	f 2.8	Fuji 100
106-107	Female Cardinal on Frosted Branch	Michigan	80-200mm w/1.4x	1/125	f 4	Fuji 100 Pushed to 200
108	First Snow	Michigan	300mm	1/250	f 2.8	Fuji 100 Pushed to 200
110	Natures Harmony	Upper Peninsula Michigan	300mm w/1.4x	1/250	f 2.8	Fuji 100
111	Wolf Pup licking Mother	Upper Peninsula Michigan	500mm	1/125	f 4	Fuji 100 Pushed to 200
112-113	Snowy Owl in Lupine	British Columbia	80-20mm	1/125	f2.8	Fuji 100 Pushed to 200
113	Dewey Damsel Fly on Blue Vervain	Michigan	200micro	1/30	f 11	K64
114	Jeannie in Canoe	Michigan	300mm w/1.4x	1/125	f 4	Fuji 100 Pushed to 200
114-115	Loons in the Mist	Michigan	300mm w/1.4x	1/125	f 4	Fuji 100 Pushed to 200
116-117	Fox in Flowers	Michigan	200micro	1/60	f 5.6	K64
117	Columbine	Michigan	105mm	1/15	f 8	K64
118-119	Crystal Mountian	Glazier NP Montana	80-200mm	1/30	f 22	Fuji 100
119	Fisher	Montana	300mm	1/30	f 2.8	Fuji 100
120	Carl with Elk	Yellowstone NP Wyoming	24mm	1/30	f 11	K64
120-121	Elk in Frosty Field	Yellowstone NP Wyoming	80-200mm	1/125	f 16	Fuji 100
122	Lower Falls from Artist Point	Yellowstone NP Wyoming	80-200mm	1/2	f 22	Fuji 100 Pushed to 200
123	Lynx in Birch	Montana	500mm	1/30	f 4	Fuji 100 Pushed to 200
124-125	Mule Deer Bucks in Grass	Canadian Rockies	80-200mm	1/250	f 2.8	Fuji 100 Pushed to 200
125	Magpie in Mule Deer Buck's Antlers	Canadian Rockies	300mm w/1.4x	1/125	f 4	Fuji 100 Pushed to 200
126	Evening Lace	Florida	500mm w/2x	1/60	f 8	Fuji 100 Pushed to 200
127	Morning Jewel	Florida	500mm w/2x	1/250	f 5.6	Fuji 100 Pushed to 200
128	Female Cardinal	Michigan	500mm	1/125	f 5.6	K64
128	Male Cardinal	Michigan	500mm	1/125	f 5.6	K64
129	White-tailed Doe in Red Leaves	Michigan	80-200mm	1/125	f 5.6	Provia
130-131	Mount McKinley	Denali NP Alaska	400mm	1/125	f 11	K64
131	Dall Sheep Ram on Ledge	by Michael Monroe	Pencil Sketch			
132	Mule Deer at Sunrise	Canadian Rockies	300mm	1/250	f 2.8	Fuji 100 Pushed to 200
133	Mountian Lion at Sunrise	Montana	300mm	1/250	f 2.8	Fuji 100 Pushed to 200
136	Mountain Sunset	Canadian Rockies	300mm	1/250	f 2.8	Fuji 100 Pushed to 200
Back Cover	Female Cardinal	Michigan	500mm	1/125	f 4	Fuji 100

PHOTOGRAPHIC PRINTS AVAILABLE

(ADDITIONAL IMAGES MAY BE AVAILABLE UPON REQUEST, CALL 1-800-552-1867)

*The warmth of the setting sun fills the heart with
expectation and the promise of the coming day.*